Magic City

Studying The Lotus Sutra
by
Ryusho Jeffus

The Magic City
Studying the Lotus Sutra

by

Ryusho Jeffus

Myosho-ji
Wonderful Voice Buddhist Temple

Wonderful Voice Publications
Charlotte, North Carolina

The Magic City

The Magic City: Studying the Lotus Sutra
By Ryusho Jeffus
Copyright 2014

Myosho-ji, Wonderful Voice Buddhist Temple
2208 Eastway Dr.
Charlotte, NC 28205

ISBN-13: 978-0692257470
ISBN-10: 0692257470

Distributed by
Wonderful Voice Publications
2208 Eastway Dr.
Charlotte, NC 28205

Contents

Introduction

There is a tradition in Jewish literature called Midrash, which briefly and perhaps over simply are the writings by scholars about what is not said in the Bible. I have recently been reading about this and thinking about some of the Lotus Sutra and what we are not told in this sacred text. At the same time these thoughts were percolating in my head I had been called upon to do some labyrinth work with several patients I worked with in the hospital. Labyrinth work is also something I employ on a weekly basis in my work with folks in detox. These two things have caused me to consider again and differently the parable of the Magic City we find in the Lotus Sutra.

Chapter VII reveals a parable that is given to us by the Buddha after much else he elaborates upon at the beginning of the chapter. This chapter is actually quite rich in teachings covering such things as a length of time since the passing of Great-Universal-Wisdom-Excellence Buddha and a description of his miracles. This leads us into the story of sixteen princes and their enlightenment. Finally we are reminded of the Four Noble Truths as well as the Twelve Causes or the Twelve Link Chain of Causation.

This is of course a rather brief account of this chapter prior to the introduction of the parable about the journey to the Magic City. The parable is being taught to the Bhiksus, those wise and learned but deeply spiritual practitioners who have removed themselves from daily life and become monks.

I find it interesting that this parable is being taught to this particular group of people. First the parable is about a group of people, the composition is unstated so we might generally imagine that it is composed of a good mixture of people; men, women, and children as well as perhaps their personal possessions. It is also a parable about traveling for personal gain or benefit. These two things could be reasonably considered outside of the normal activities of those individuals who have removed themselves from worldly pursuits and certainly from travel for personal gain. There might even be a case to be made that monks would not even begin such a journey in the normal set of circumstances.

Of course there is the symbolic meaning which we traditionally ascribe to this parable that the journey, the guide, the interval at the Magic City are all metaphors for the spiritual journey a monk or even a lay person. The traditional way of interpreting this parable leaves a lot of things unspoken and also somewhat detaches it from how we actually live our daily lives. I also feel the traditional interpretation limits the implications and the value of this parable to us the modern practitioner.

Purposefully examining this parable and many of the unstated things can actually teach us much about many aspects of our living and embracing the Lotus Sutra, and I believe can bring this parable to life in the modern age with many implications for the sorts of things we face daily.

So, with that let's dig in and see what we come up with

Before the Journey

"I will tell you a parable. Once upon a time there was a dangerous, bad road five hundred yojanas long. It was so fearful that no men lived in the neighborhood. Now many people wished to pass through this road in order to reach a place of treasures." (Chapter VII, page 226)

"Suppose there was a bad and dangerous road.
Many wild animals lived in the neighborhood.
No man was there; no water nor grass there.
The road was so fearful.

Many tens of millions of people
Wished to pass through this dangerous road.
The road was very long.
It was five hundred yojanas long."
(Lotus Sutra, Chapter VII, page 234)

As I mentioned in the Introduction depending upon how you think about the parable it can be somewhat strange that it was given to monks, especially since it is about moving, traveling, and seeking unlimited treasures. Yes, these are symbols but I do think that symbols are more effective if they actually relate to the person or event. Yet, there is a connection in this though not necessarily in the traditionally used interpretation.

First though let us look at the traditional interpretation. It is generally thought and taught simply that the unlimited wealth is Anuttara-samyak-sambodhi, and the journey along the road is the practice of Buddhism. But the symbols used to represent this are not ones that are traditionally applied to monastics at the time of this parable, or even generally any time.

For us though as practitioners who are not monastic the imagery is quite appropriate. Think about your own personal journeys to magic cities. These could be going to college so you learn a trade or skill that will enable you to support yourself during your life. Or the journey may be the search to find a new job. The journey might include courting a partner during a romantic relationship towards perhaps a long term commitment. It may also be the raising of a child either with a partner or by one's self. There are in fact many journeys we embark upon daily, such as our journey in to work at the beginning of our shift.

This may on the surface seem to be taking this parable lightly but bear with me if you will. It is very important the way we proceed with every activity of life, because how we begin determines how we end. The way we start any activity greatly influences the outcome or the way it ends. The causes we make are the determiner of the effects we receive. So considering our many, perhaps infinite, journeys throughout our lifetime is a practical activity for Buddhists.

On a personal level do you consider how you begin something? In the hospital where I work as a chaplain we begin every day in community spending a few minutes as we each share our intentions for the day and for the work we are about to engage in. Setting one's intention either as we start an activity or as we engage in the activity can help remind us what it is we really hope to accomplish. I am not sure about how your day goes but it is easy to jump right in to work and bounce around from task to task. Sometimes that works and other times I am left feeling somewhat scattered or even doubtful that I did my best. Stating my intention in the morning encourages me to seek some mental clarity and focus so that I am more inclined to use my energies in the way I would wish. It also allows me to name, honor and listen to any turmoil that may potentially hinder my intentions.

In the parable the travelers knew where they wanted to go. They have, as we are told, the goal of traveling to a place of unlimited treasure. For us unlimited treasure exists on many levels. It can be a treasure of satisfaction knowing that you accomplished what you set out to do, and you did it well, skillfully and with mindfulness. But we cannot expect to act mindfully if we don't begin mindfully. And part of mindfulness is actually knowing where we wish to go.

But how do these people know about the place of unlimited treasure? We aren't told how they found out about it. When I think back to my early days of Buddhist practice, I was merely seeking Buddhism in a general way, because from what I knew about it it closely aligned with my basic beliefs. Now perhaps you were more sophisticated, but over the years it has been my experience that most people approach Buddhism initially with a very limited view of the possibilities, practice, or theory. Over time they learn and grow, just as I too learned and grew.

When I began practicing Buddhism, and this has been my observation in others, the goal isn't necessarily enlightenment but most frequently it is the resolution of some life crisis or perhaps some direction. In other words for most of us when we started our practice the place of unlimited treasure isn't even on our horizon, heck we aren't even looking for a magic illusionary city. And yet if we scale it down, that is in fact what we are doing when we tackle our smaller problems, we are seeking an 'unlimited treasure'. Think how much $10 means to a person who is flat out broke, hungry, and trying really hard to make it but just not succeeding. That $10 may seem insignificant to many but to that person it is indeed priceless and extremely valuable, even an unlimited treasure.

I believe that as we read the Lotus Sutra we should not approach it as stories or parables about someone other than our very own selves. In fact these aren't even stories about us or about anyone, they are in fact our very lives as they are as Buddhas or Buddhists. As long as we externalize or fantasize about Buddhism and fail to realize that the Lotus Sutra is really about us, you, me, anyone and everyone who seeks to embrace, practice and believe in the teachings of the Buddha, then we aren't getting the message, we aren't Buddhists in a sense. The more we can become the stories and the better able we are at identifying ourselves in the Lotus Sutra the closer we become to awakening to our enlightenment.

We are not told in the parable specifically how it is these people came together it just says many people. Judging by the text they traveled together so how did they manage to hook up with each other? What motivated them?

We can of course say that they represent the Bhiksus and their quest for enlightenment, but how can we read this in our own lives? Consider if you will the question as it relates to your own journey into and in Buddhism. How is it that you developed a seeking or questing to learn and practice Buddhism? What was or is going on in your life that draws you to your practice and motivates you to continue day after day?

I am sure that many if not all of us at some point have been asked why we began practicing Buddhism. I know I myself and continually asked this question. The question I am asking here is not about the events necessarily that led you to practice, but what was going on in your self at your core that really was at the heart of your searching out of Buddhism or your willingness to try it out. I suppose it is possible that there may be someone out there who just did it entirely on a whim. Someone who just by random circumstances found themselves at a Sangha activity and for no reason what so ever decided to do something completely different for no other reason than...well for no reason at all.

Most of us though, if we look deeply back at that time, could find some underlying reason. For myself, on the one hand I could say I began practicing Buddhism because in high school I read something that made a lot of sense; short story. But really deeper down was a deep sense of helplessness. I was in the Marine Corps, very unhappy, feeling alone in my beliefs, despondent even. When I went to my first Sangha meeting the room was full of 20 other Marines all chanting Odaimoku together. Afterwards as they spoke of their beliefs and about Buddhism I felt at home, at peace, welcomed, embraced and a lot more. Mostly though I felt hopeful. I felt there was hope after all, that things could be different, and things could even be better. Those were some of the core reasons why I sought out Buddhism, why I went to my first activity, and why I decided to continue. I really, honestly wasn't motivated nor thinking about enlightenment. I just wanted to be happy.

At this point as part of the practice of this parable of the Magic City it would be very beneficial to engage in some personal exploration. We don't talk much in Buddhism about discernment. But without discerning where we are and where we wish to go, we will not truly be able to know how to begin, where to begin or what will need to be done in order to become happy and attain enlightenment. We'll talk more about guides, directions and so forth. For now spend some time in introspection on the reasons you began the search for and the practice of Buddhism.

In philosophy circles there is a technical term used to talk about a belief in something. It isn't possible to believe in something for which you know nothing about, at least from a philosophical stand point. Belief is discussed in terms of intentionality, but here the term has a more complicated meaning than merely intention. For the lay person, and please understand that I am one of those lay people, since I am not a philosopher, the term aboutness is substituted to enable us to get a better understanding of what belief is.

If we think about belief in Buddhism there really isn't any belief until we become about something. Simply saying 'I believe in Buddhism' has no fundamental meaning, it is empty. It doesn't have meaning until there is something we are actually engaging in to manifest that belief or until we become about Buddhism.

This is arguable of course but beyond the point I wish to make. At what point do we transfer a liking or agreeing with Buddhist thoughts and ideas into actually becoming Buddhist in our aboutness? Buddhism itself then becomes the 'place of unlimited treasures' though we can hardly say that at the very beginning we knew how unlimited or even what those treasures were. Over time those treasures we seek change and mutate, some may even disappear because we are no longer interested in such things. How have things changed for you over the course of your practice?

There is also the idea that your aboutness changes over time as you yourself change and as your belief changes. Ideally the changes are accompanied by both intellectual knowledge and actual changes in your life. The more areas of your life that are affected by Buddhism the more you become about Buddhism, and so you in a sense become more Buddhist. But you really aren't Buddhist until you become about Buddhism or until your Buddhist aboutness manifests.

In the course of your life you face the beginning of many journeys, not all of which are thought of as spiritual. Going of to college, beginning a new job, getting married, having children, and retiring are some of the many types of new adventures you might engage in sometimes several times in one lifetime. Some of these activities you may just jump right in with little or no forethought, and others you may actually think long and deeply about. Sometimes you may be faced with making decisions about something with preparation and other times it is thrust upon you with no warning.

Making choices in life may lead you closer to your goal and at other times you may find yourself being propelled further and further from your desired objective. Labyrinths are like this. As you walk the path there are times when you are so very close to the center and then before you know it your path takes you way far away to the outer edge. It seems at time as if you are further from your goal than you ever were, when you began. Yet this is merely an illusion because your path is growing ever shorter and your destination is becoming ever closer. This twisting path you follow on your journey is deceptive and can throw you into crisis sometimes. You may even consider stepping over the lines to either exit or to take a short cut to the center. Every short cut you take, though, robs you of experiences that may in fact prove valuable and necessary at some other point on in your traveling the road of life.

When you finally decided to explore or even practice Buddhism can you recall what it was that really convinced you to take up the faith in earnest? This awakening may not have occurred at the very outset, it may have occurred later on. Also, your awakening may have occurred numerous times over the years of your practice. There may have been times when you reached new plateaus of faith, or of aboutness.

Let us return to the parable, shall we. One thing we are not told is how these people came together. How was it they found each other, or decided collectively to undertake this journey?

The men who put the Lotus Sutra into written words were almost certainly very spiritual beings. These were undoubtedly men whose whole lives were devoted to and immersed in Buddhism. Their aboutness is probably about as complete as we can imagine. For these men, trying to explain their spiritual experiences and awakening was I can imagine a difficult endeavor. Heck for me to even explain what I experience when I chant Odaimoku or read the sutra is diminished by words. Words of our languages will always fall short when trying to describe our spiritual experiences.

When words fall short we rely on symbols, codes, and shorthand. Spiritual writers of the Lotus Sutra were no different and challenged as equally as all the creators of all of the spiritual and sacred texts of man's many religions. The Lotus Sutra is no exception in its use of symbols, codes, and shorthand. That is why, I believe, that a story such as this parable leaves out much the authors assumed we would understand.

Yet, here we are some 2000 years later, a time that I am guessing is almost infinitely in the future for these men. Think about it for a moment. Can you even begin to imagine what the world will be like in another 2000 years? There are many science fiction writers who have imagined future times. Some of these times are idyllic and some are dystopian full of all sorts of nightmares of technology, people, and climate run amuck. I think back 20 years in my life and the changes I have seen have been so dramatic and unimaginable it calls into question any claim I might have to seeing into the future.

These men though, were less concerned with the everyday and so set aside their need to tailor a message for the future. Instead what they strove to do was write something that would be timeless, and almost independent of any external factors. And so this parable is able to speak to us across time with an applicability that transcends our individual circumstances.

Considering this for a moment you might ask yourself the age old question of whether you are a spiritual being living an ordinary life or an ordinary person living a spiritual life? This is important because it questions whether you see being spiritual as something removed from catching the commuter train in the morning and riding to work shoulder to shoulder with others engaged in the same activity. What I am proposing to you is that shopping at your favorite grocery store, gathering your groceries, standing in line at the checkout counter, loading your purchase into your car and then driving home to put them away is no less an opportunity to have a spiritual experience than those moments you sit in front of your altar and recite the sutra or chant Odaimoku.

The decisions you make about which job to apply for or which person to be in relationship, or which school to place your children into are no less spiritual than seeking enlightenment or traveling to the place of unlimited treasures. I also propose to you that frequently it isn't the actual decision you make that is as important as it is the manner in which you engage in those activities.

When I was originally mulling around how to write this and what I might cover some images that came into my mind were things like the Jews fleeing Nazi Germany, the people who fled Rwanda, or even the crisis in Syria occurring now, or the Mormons as they moved and settled in Utah, or the early pioneers traveling across this huge country of ours, or the fabled Pilgrims of early America. In each instance what these all have in common and what we share also in our daily activities is a need or reason to do something, a search for the thing to do or in these examples a place to go, finding a way to do or go, and somcone to tiusl who will guide them.

The Guide

"They were led by a man, clever, wise, and well informed of the conditions of the dangerous road." (Lotus Sutra, Chapter VII, page 226)

"The people had a leader.
He had a good memory.
He was wise and resolute in mind.
He could save people from dangers."
(Lotus Sutra, Chapter VII, page 234)

Even as you apply for a job you require people you can trust, folks who can give you advice in how to prepare a resume or conduct an interview. We all need someone else in order to succeed. There really is no truly self-made person. It is said the blacksmith is unique among tradesmen because he can make his own tools. Yet it has been the rare case of the blacksmith who minded his own ore. Even a test-tube baby needs a mother for now and always someone to feed and nourish them.

So you make your decision using your set of criteria for your own individual reasons but how do you decide upon who will guide you? How did you decide that practicing the Lotus Sutra was or is the correct path for you to follow? If you were merely seeking out Buddhism in general, there are countless ways in which to engage in Buddhist practice and develop your Buddhist aboutness. What was it about the Lotus Sutra that caught your attention?

When I think about the parable I wonder what criteria those travelers used to determine that their guide was worthy of their trust. Looking at examples throughout history the one that comes immediately to my mind are the stories of refugees fleeing war zones, or even the Jews fleeing Germany. I often wonder how people find the person they need to lead them safely. Here in the US there are countless stories of people who cross the boarder from Mexico who hook up with an unscrupulous person who takes them out onto the desert then steals their money and leaves them to die of heat and thirst.

I once knew a young Mexican boy (from my age he was a boy, but he was actually a young man) who worked near where I worked. He was one of the cooks. I would always great all the cooks and talk to them trying to get to know the person, who they were, and what their story was. In this case this young man would return home twice a year to visit his family in the central part of Mexico. He would tell me about his journey. It seems the trip home to Mexico is fairly easy and safe. But the return trip is very dangerous. He had made the trip so many times that he was reasonably confident that he was as safe as he could be on the journey.

How do people make such life and death decisions? I cannot imagine the fear and the difficulty of making those kind of choices. It would be even more frightful if there were other family members such as children you were responsible for. Sometimes, especially in war zones there really isn't much time to make a decision, you just have to act and pray for the best.

We aren't told these circumstances apply to the travelers in the Magic City. It could be the case that just as many people cross our boarder with Mexico in search of economic advantage these people in the parable are also looking to improve their situation in life out of desperation.

Thinking about your own life, have there been times when you have had to make a very important decision? What criteria did you use to base your decision? I think back to what was may have been the most important decision I ever made and I guess I didn't have any criteria other than a gut check. That decision was about going to a Buddhist meeting with a stranger whom I knew nothing about other than he was a senior enlisted man. My choice at the time was whether suicide was an option. As I mentioned this was a very low point in my life. I am not sure I would have carried out suicide but I had never thought so much about it or as seriously as I did at that time. Here I was gay, in the Marine Corps, possibly facing going into combat in Vietnam. It was hell for me. I had already been living away from home since I was in college so it wasn't being away from home that was part of my despondency; it was I simply was the wrong person for the place I found myself in.

I saw no way out and no way to change things. I didn't want to kill anyone and I didn't want to die. On top of that I had to hide who I was because it wasn't safe; I couldn't let anyone find out I was gay. So along comes this guy asking if anyone wants to go to a Buddhist meeting. What did I have to loose? I went and there has been no turning back for me since that night in 1969.

In Chapter XVI the Buddha talks about how people with mistaken views think the world is in a great fire when in actuality it is peaceful. If we think the world is a great fire then on one level each of us is fleeing the raging fires of greed, ignorance, and anger. Buddhism becomes our safe refuge from all of the sufferings of life. We are always to some degree or another refugees from suffering seeking peace and security.

How do you decide among frequently many options which course of action to take? Do you have any basic criteria, or do you just wing it? What is your method of problem solving, have you even ever considered it?

When it came to my deciding to practice Nichiren Buddhism my first criteria was simply did it make sense and was it believable. I was not looking for something magical that would take all of my problems away from me and fortunately I wasn't offered that on my first night exposed to the Lotus Sutra. What I heard made sense and put simply, it agreed with many things I had intuited over the years. Later I came to learn about actual and theoretical proof. Does it make sense, and does it work? Simple but quite effective.

Recently I was approached by three different individuals with different offers of employment as a Chaplain. You would think this would not be crisis producing, and yet it did throw me into a weekend of internal turmoil. Without going into all the details I'll simply say that over the course of several days I internally worked through what my values were, what was important to me at this point in my life, identifying the complications that were causing me grief and were not really directly related to my decision and were merely clouding the landscape, casting a fog if you will, and taking the risk to fail.

As I've mentioned I am reading an interesting book on the philosophy of philosophy. The book is discussing several tools we can use to increase our intuition and work through solving problems. It just so happened that on that same weekend I was reading about the value and importance of failure.

The author posits that in this day and age we have become a culture averse to failure and yet it is in failure we have the greatest potential for learning and growing. His claim is that by always taking the safe option sometimes we miss our greatest opportunities and frequently we even fail to act out of this fear. He reminds his readers that it rarely happens that the earth opens up and swallows a person whole simply because they made a mistake or failed at something.

Of course there are times when our decisions are very important and can impact our lives and futures in very significant ways. So we do need to do due diligence in our decision making. But always living in fear is as if the travelers who wished to go the place of unlimited treasures never actually went anywhere and instead stayed home.

According to the parable in the sutra the man was clever, wise, and well informed. I am also guessing that the man came with good references, though the sutra doesn't mention that specifically. In the gatha section these additional traits are mentioned. He had a good memory, he was resolute in mind, meaning he had a strong determination and would not be deterred easily, and he could save the people.

Now we have a pretty good idea of the characteristics of the person these travelers looked for in the leader they would choose. I don't see anything wrong with their criteria, do you?

As I was thinking about this, and perhaps influenced by some of my patient encounters as a chaplain, the idea of how frequently we have very good mental intentions yet when put into practice we sometimes fall short of our ideals. It is very difficult sometimes to live up to our own highest expectations. I am not sure about you, but for me that is frequently frustrating or even severely disappointing.

My work on the detox unit has led me to many encounters with patients trying to overcome their addictions who fall short of their goals. Also I am in frequent contact with individuals who in spite of their desires to eat better, quit smoking, exercise, manage their diabetes, and so forth fall short of their expectations and their known ideals. Are there places in your life where you experience a discord between what you know you should do, or you want to do and what you actually end up doing?

If, however, you are like most people, there are probably areas where you don't live up to your greatest expectations. What do we do in situations like this? Giving up is of course one possible way of dealing with it. There is another way forward though, and that is to continue to strive to reach your dream. My work with folks in detox puts me in contact with many people who are on their third or fourth attempt at living clean and or sober. One of the catch phrases this group uses is you have to keep trying and that when you finally reach your bottom it will stick but keep trying until then.

Well, that's actually not such a bad way to approach your life goals, no matter what they may be. Now this is going to sound silly but I used to bite my finger nails. I did this until I was about 50 years old. There were many times when I didn't care about whether I bit them or not, but most of the time it was embarrassing and I wanted to quit. I tried many things to stop but nothing worked. Finally though I was able to quit when I got a new job in sales where I was constantly out meeting people trying to sell printing services. I just realized it wasn't very professional looking having nails chewed down to the quick. When I ran a printing press it didn't seem to matter as much because no one really saw my nails.

In a sense I reached my low point and was finally able to stop biting my nails. The unfortunate thing was that by this time because of the years of biting and ripping my nails when they grew out some were slightly deformed. So I suffered permanent damage as a result of my previous actions. Life is like that frequently; we cannot completely escape effect of previous causes.

Getting back to our story, the leader they chose was resolute in mind. As we learn later in the parable, this was an important character trait. When the group of travelers became discouraged and wanted to quit the leader kept them going and enabled them through his resolute determination to reach their desired destination. Sometimes even when our own determination is not enough we need the support of true resolute friends.

Seeking out people of wisdom as we go through our lives is extremely important. The other day I was speaking with a friend and we were talking about people who have influenced us in positive ways and we will always remember.

When I got my first real job it was working in a grocery store as a cashier and bag boy. I shall always remember the manager, Mr. Anderson. His motto was, and he would say it all the time, "no one is too good to push a broom." There were several of us part-timers who were in high school together and we worked there almost like a family. Since we all went to the same high school and we were all in the same grade we all wanted the same nights off. Of course that wouldn't work out because who would work the store. He was very fair about it though, and he kept a list of who had what days off and he would rotate us around. We all thought he treated us nicely and ever yone of us would go to the end of the earth for him. My only complaint was he always picked on me to get my haircut; he didn't want any hippies working the cash register. Years later after I had moved away my mother would give him a hard time when he followed fashion trends eventually and let his sideburns grow as well as his hair got a little longer too.

I learned a lot from that man, as well as many others at various times in my life. I think it is important to realize that sometimes we may need different people in our lives for different reasons. I think it is important though to discern which people are helping us grow and which people are hindering our development. And this has nothing to do with whether someone is nice, or fun, or entertaining.

In a way you need to be wise enough to find a wise person appropriate to your needs. The travelers in our parable had the wisdom you could say to choose wisely a wise person for their particular needs. Who are some of the wise people you have had in your life?

Of course it was important their leader have a good memory because he would need to be able to remember where the treacherous portions of the road were, where to find water, when would it be appropriate to spend the night and so on. For your particular needs you may have a different or similar set of criteria but in any case I do think it wise to know what your resources are and where to find what you need.

The teachings of the Buddha provide an excellent example of instruction, compassion, and resolution which can be used by anyone at any time in any situation. Buddhism is benefiting many people throughout the world. I know why I continue to follow the teachings of the Buddha but I wonder what motivates you to keep going?

A question I frequently ask people in the hospital who have received some unfortunate news and who are faced with an unexpected crisis is; 'What has gotten you through the tough times in the past?' When any of us are faced with some difficult situation we should look to our past to see what helped us and what perhaps was not so skillful. One of my personal ideas about being a chaplain is how can I either reconnect someone with their spiritual foundation if they are in doubt, or how can I facilitate someone to find solace in some spiritual path that speaks to their heart.

One of the reasons I write all that I do is because I am unable to speak directly to many people, not nearly as many as read my books or follow my blog. I write with the hope that you will create such an intimate relationship with the Buddha and the Lotus Sutra that abandoning your faith would be the last thing you would think about doing in a crisis situation. There is no way of knowing what situations you will face in your life. However, if you have a strong connection with the Lotus Sutra you will have a guide who can see you through the rough road you need to travel to your happiness.

Thinking about our travelers once they have committed to following the guide and have begun their journey they have limited their options for changing their minds. Just imagine you are in a wagon train driving from Missouri to, oh I don't know, let's say California. Well, by the time you are a week out on the journey you as an individual wagon probably would not survive if you turned around by yourself and tried to go home. If you are being smuggled out of your country into another you will not be highly thought of if in the middle of the night you decide to quit the trip and get up and turn around risking discovery of the entire group.

You can of course abandon your Buddhist practice at any point in your life, you can walk away and there is no retribution for doing so. Unlike many religions that teach punishment or retribution, Buddhism isn't spreading that message. You are free at any point to proceed with the rest of your life in any way you deem best. It is my hope though that you will choose to continue you Buddhist practice for the long haul.

Give yourself 10 years. I know, who the heck wants to wait around 10 years for something? Heck we go to the nursery and by full grown trees simply because we want an instant landscape. Still, 10 years is a fair time in which for you to measure your life growth. I mean, you are going to live that 10 years anyway, why not add some spice to your life and live the 10 years with as much Buddhist aboutness as you possibly can, following our good leader and guide The Buddha, traveling with our many Sangha friends.

Before I finish with this pre-journey stuff I wanted to talk about some of the modern journey stories. Joseph Campbell has called these, the hero's journey. In a way I think we all can call ourselves heroes and we are certainly on a journey. There are lessons we can learn from the heroic journeys of myth and legend, and this parable is one example. What lessons can you learn from this or other heroic journeys?

Perhaps I should define a hero from the perspective of the Lotus Sutra and Buddhism. Understanding what a hero is can help us better see that we are in fact mighty heroes of our time even when the rest of the world may measure things in terms of wealth and success, heroism is measured differently in Buddhism.

Nichiren Shonin says in a letter to one of his followers, Shijo Kingo, "Buddhism primarily concerns itself with victory or defeat, while secular authority is based on the principle of reward and punishment [win or lose]. For this reason, a Buddha is looked up to as the Hero of the World".

Let's examine the meaning of the word hero. There are many meanings that are attributed to this word, some of which have to do with gods. I would like to set those aside as not being applicable in this instance. The literal meaning of the word is "protector", "defender" or "guardian". In this case we might look to characters, fictional or historical, who in the face of danger and adversity or from a position of weakness, display courage and the will for self-sacrifice; that is, heroism.

Fundamentally in life there is no winning or losing. We are not in a competition with others nor with ourselves when it comes to enlightenment or happiness. When we fail to accomplish a goal or some aspiration we are not losers. That is, we are not losers or defeated unless we allow ourselves to be so. But it is a choice, and one that only we can choose.

Fifty years ago Willie O'Ree became the first black man to play for a professional hockey team. It had been his life long dream to play professional hockey. Growing up in Canada he lived and breathed hockey. As if the challenge of being the first black man in professional hockey wasn't enough, he was also blind in one eye.

Before his professional career began he was injured when a hockey puck hit him in the eye. According to him it never occurred to him to not play. This is victory. To not be defeated by obstacles in one's life is not a matter of winning or losing it is whether or not you allow yourself to be defeated. And even if you don't achieve your ultimate goal, if you never give up, you will achieve something worthwhile none-the-less. Every effort to achieve a goal we set is valuable and should not be discounted. Even if in the end we do not meet our goal or achieve our expectation, we still have the result of our effort.

In the chapter Parable of a Magic City in the Lotus Sutra it says, "You, the Hero of the World, are unequalled. Adorned with the marks of one hundred merits, you have obtained unsurpassed wisdom. Expound the Dharma and save us and other living beings of the world!"

Why is the Buddha called "hero of the world"? The Buddha defeated the evil forces of Mara and began to teach the dharma in order to save all living beings. The Buddha achieved victory over his own self and his own self-doubt. The Buddha was not in a competition with any one. He was not competing with the other ascetics; if he had been he would never have abandoned those practices and followed the middle way. The Buddha was not concerned with winning a competition, which would have only exhibited selfish qualities, thinking of his own status. Instead, with no regard for the appearance of things he abandoned ascetic practice and attained enlightenment. Even beyond that he didn't keep his enlightenment to himself, instead he sought to share his victory with others.

In our own lives all too often we are mislead with notions of winning and losing. We miss the larger important concept of victory and defeat. We compare ourselves with other things or people judging our success by standards that do not truly reflect our own accomplishments.

I encourage each of you to re-examine your lives and your thinking. Ask yourself if you are valuing your life from the perspective of victory or from winning? Do you truly value all of your experiences and efforts from the perspective that no effort in Buddhism is wasted? If you are only concerned with winning and losing then I think you may tend to discount your efforts when they seem to fall short. On the other hand if you are concerned with victory or defeat then you can shift your thinking to look at all of your efforts as contributing in some way to your personal growth.

Becoming enlightened is not about winning some competition against something or someone. It is about overcoming your own suffering and leading by example. Becoming enlightened is about becoming victorious over illusion, victorious over suffering, victorious over self-doubt, and becoming victorious in life.

Reflecting on this a little deeper it occurs to me to ask a couple of questions. Does the hero find the guide or the guide find the hero? Which is really the hero, the guide or the one making the journey?

Two stories from contemporary fiction come immediately to my mind. One is the story told to us in Lord of the Rings, the other is more recent and that is Harry Potter. As I write this a third one comes to mind and that is Star Wars, but I am not as familiar with that one, it never really spoke to me, perhaps because it was mainly a movie event and I do not watch many movies.

In Harry Potter and Lord of the Rings the guide finds the hero but the guide is also heroic in their own right. The heroic guide though does not overshadow the journeyer, and the guide hero is ultimately very altruistic in giving to the journeyer.

These two stories interest me also because I wonder why we can trust the guide since they often do not reveal the whole truth and keep things hidden from the journeyer. Gandalf and Dumbledore are likable enough characters with a lot of charm and charisma but they also can be seen as somewhat self-serving at times.

It isn't my intent to do an in-depth analysis of fiction literature but they do offer some contrast to our parable in the Lotus Sutra. In the parable we aren't really told how the people came to be associated with their guide. If you are like me you may have assumed they went looking for their guide, but the sutra does not say that. It simply says they were led by, or had a leader. We don't know how they found each other.

There have been times in my life when I have wondered whether I found the Lotus Sutra or it found me. It is certainly the case that I was interested in Buddhism and had an inclination to want to practice. Yet in actuality I was somewhat passive about which kind of Buddhism, the Lotus Sutra came to me, though it was incumbent upon me to take advantage of the opportunity.

I think also about the many people who reach out to me via the web and say they are interested in practicing Nichiren Buddhism and the Lotus Sutra but in the end don't actually do anything other than say they are interested. It is as if they wish to travel to some place of unlimited treasure, find a guide but never pack their bags and step outside the door and make the journey "there and back again." This is perhaps why the Buddha praises so highly anyone who asks him questions seeking to deepen their understanding of Buddhism and especially those who continue to do so three or more times.

You are the hero of your own story and how heroic you are depends entirely upon yourself. The Buddha can be your guide and the Lotus Sutra can be your map, but ultimately you and you alone must make the journey necessary to your own enlightenment. Every nanosecond of your life is a manifestation of your spiritual self though we sometimes may wish to ignore the oneness.

This parable has so many implications and offers many truths to an infinite number of instances in our daily lives.

The Journey

"He took them along this dangerous road, but halfway the people got tired of walking. They said to him, 'We are tired out. We are also afraid of the danger of this road. We cannot go a step farther. Our destination is still far off. We wish to go back." (Lotus Sutra, Chapter VII, page 226)

"Getting tired,
The people said to him:
"We are tired.
We wish to go back." (Lotus Sutra, Chapter VII, page 224)

Have you ever considered the role your obstacles play in your growth and movement to enlightenment? Reflecting again on the two fictional heroes of Frodo and Harry Potter we see the necessity of a nemesis to the actual success of the journey. Frodo needs Gollum and Harry needs Snape. Also in both stories these two relative villains are not purely bad, and both have been formed through events early in their lives which they are acting through to the very end. Gollum set into motion his downward spiral by killing his friend out of jealousy to acquire the found ring. Snape is greatly influenced by being outcast and teased by Harry's father.

Our group of merry travelers in the parable are motivated to seek out their guide because of the difficulties they anticipate facing. We are only told of their motivation to travel because they wished to go to a place of unlimited treasures, or for their self-improvement. Beyond that we have no information about possibly other reasons why such a large group wishes the leave the place in which they live.

In our lives we do not normally seek to change, change for most people is upsetting at the least and traumatic at worst. It is, for most of us, our natural inclination to avoid change. We like things to be familiar, predictable, comfortable, which of course means that we are more inclined to stagnate and also suffer. Not everyone is this way of course but generally this is true. Is this true for you? Honestly?

One of my favorite expressions is "nothing remains unchanged forever." Every situation, every person, every everything is constantly in flux, is constantly changing. Our own lives are ever moving towards eventual death and decay. Along that journey we may be joyful or we may be in agony. It is our Buddhist practice that can assist in being able to experience the joy amidst the uncertainty, loss, and change. Not only are we changing, others are changing as well.

When you think about all of the potential possibilities in any given moment it is a wonder you don't go crazy trying to position yourself to be in the best situation possible. In fact it is impossible to be one hundred percent correct all of the time with absolute certainty and with no possibility of being wrong. You may indeed be successful many times but in a way that is more coincidence than any true skill on your part. It can be pretty scary.

Even if you successfully predict the rise of a certain stock on the stock market you might be unexpectedly diagnosed with a fatal cancer. Something is always out there as a potential to blind side you when you least expect it.

Of course you generally operate under the assumption that nothing bad or unexpected will happen. Normally you have a defense mechanism that your ancestors either evolved with or had originally that keeps you from dwelling continually on all the negative possibilities. Not everyone though has this trait, and perhaps you have known someone such as this. If you are one of those I hope that you are seeking out professional help beyond your Buddhist practice, taking advantage of science to assist you in normalizing your necessary defenses against going crazy with fear.

It is because of the expectation that you are in control of events in your lives and the hope that things will not change unless we make them that you leave yourself open to suffering. No one can avoid pain, change, decay, and death to name a few. What you can do however is lessen your grasping for these to never happen. Buddhism teaches us of impermanence. Your work as a Buddhist is to understand the implications of this in your life and in your happiness. It isn't easy, this is your hero's journey.

You may be sitting there right about now and thinking, 'gosh this is depressing' or 'my my aren't you the pessimistic one'. I do not believe this is pessimistic thinking or depressing, especially not when you consider the truth of change. Change is actually the most predictable thing in your life. When you operate with the clear understanding of change you actually are in effect much more in control of your potential to manage suffering.

I believe managing change is perhaps the second big reason for the existence of religions. Death is the first and even that is fundamentally a condition of change. So perhaps change is the only reason for any religion. Managing and controlling change, or even preventing change can be found at the root of most if not all religious practices and teachings; Buddhism is in that regard no different. We just approach it from a different direction. Rather than controlling change we try to open ourselves up to the reality that change happens to every thing and not grasp for an unchanging reality. What are you clinging to that may be causing suffering?

The Parable of the Magic City is classic change management.

At the very beginning of the story the people are seeking to change their circumstances by changing their location. Because of the danger of the road they seek to manage that by changing the odds to their favor by seeking out a guide. They further try to manage the potential for change by selecting someone of superior qualities. In this next section they are tired, their individual life condition has changed from when they began and now they wish to manage that change by turning around.

We are a very controlling species are we not? We tend to want things on our own terms on our own schedule. We cling very tightly to ourselves.

Of the two reasons given to us as to why the travelers wished to return home I would like to touch upon their becoming tired out at the half way point. Also I am curious about the changes they may have experienced in their group during the time they have traveled so far.

From the parable we know the length of the journey as being 500 yojanas long. Yojana is both a measurement of distance as well as time. Simply stated a yojana is the distance an ox-cart can travel in one day. As carts improved in construction and roads also improved the distance grew but it was still a measurement of days. So we know the total length of the journey to the fabled city was to take 500 days. That is almost a year and a half, a lot can happen in that length of time.

I wonder how many babies were born during that time, as surely there must have been unless everyone abstained from sex for the nine months before the journey as well as the entire length of the journey. This is highly unlikely. So amidst our group of travelers there almost certainly must have been a child born, or two or three. Perhaps even some may have died along the trip as well.

I think about some of the mass movements of people across the plains of the US. Back in the time of the gold rush, a trip to a place of unimaginable fabled wealth, the trip from the East Coast to California would take almost a year. Part of the trip was traveling to the staging point of St. Louis where groups would form and then head out across the plains and mountains in covered wagons. There were many births and deaths along that journey.

It is I suspect impossible for a span of even a year to pass much less a year and a half without some possibly significant changes in a person's life to occur.

Every year at the beginning of the New Year as part of the services at my temple I pass around sheets of blank paper, envelopes, and pens. I then make time for people to write their goals for the upcoming year on the blank paper. Then that is sealed in the envelope with their address written of the front. I collect the envelopes and place them on the altar and on the first of July I mail them out to those who took part. The reason I do this is to provide a reminder to people of what their goals were at the beginning of the year and perhaps allow them to reassess where they are and where they wish to go in regard to their personal growth.

I wonder if you remember what your goals are for this year. Do you, as part of your life process, make personal goals, listing things you wish to achieve over periods of time? If it is not something you do how accurately are you able to really assess your growth and change. Merely going through life, with no clear direction and no clear idea from where you began makes it extremely difficult to determine the path of change and growth or lack thereof.

Of course if you have a major life event, such as the birth of child or the death of a family member, that is an easy demarcation in your life. A new job or the loss of a job also provides an easy comparison. Yet many of the changes that are fundamental to our long-term happiness, the changes our lives make as we progress towards enlightenment, are subtle and imperceptible to us on a day-to-day basis. Frequently it is only when we look back with a clear picture of where we were and where we are presently that we can see how much our lives have changed.

The travelers on their 500-day journey may have thought the journey would never end. Without the ability to look back over what they had covered and how much remained I can imagine it would be discouraging. I have had people come to me for encouragement because they feel they have not made any progress.

If I know the person well enough I can sometimes tell them about what their life was like a year ago or remind them of the great changes that indeed have occurred in their lives. It isn't always the case that I am able to do this. Regardless, I always encourage people to step back away from examining their lives one day at a time and look at a summary of days. On a day-to-day basis it almost always is the case that our lives have ups and downs. But over time, as we work on changing our lives at the core, and as we work to make significant change in our life to attain enlightenment, we can see a steady incline towards the positive. It might not be a smooth upward increase, it almost certainly will be jagged, but the general trend will be to the positive, especially if we develop a consistent practice.

If, though, you have no clear awareness of where you were when you began, and have no goal to completion then determining where you came from, where you are going, and were you are presently in relation is very difficult if not perhaps impossible. Constant reflection, reexamination, reassessment is part of the process of growth; otherwise we tend to wander aimlessly.

I wonder what you could accomplish in your life if you made a commitment from today for 500 days to practice on a regular consistent basis towards the achievement of some change in your life? Would you be able to travel the entire 500 days without giving up or abandoning or forgetting your goal and effort? Most people over the course of one year are unable to follow through on their yearly determination and even many people do not even bother setting out a list of goals for the year. It is no wonder that we may feel as if we are not changing, or as if we are unable to accomplish our dreams. The path to enlightenment is a life-long journey, one year or 500 days is simply a small portion of that journey. I hope that you can make a renewed determination after reading this to establish some goals for yourself and make effort towards accomplishing them.

Elsewhere I have written about one of my goals to study Buddhism when I first converted. When I was very new in the practice I made this goal and it continues to this day. When I first started out I didn't know much about Buddhism but I wanted to learn. There was so much for me to accomplish it seemed impossible. At that time I was encouraged to read and study twenty minutes a day.

Twenty minutes is not very much. You may think that there isn't much value in such a short period of study. At the time I was in the US Marine Corps and for me twenty minutes was a big chunk of time. Time was in short supply during much of my service. Sometimes there would be nights when I would be called back to work so I was never sure if I would get any time to study. Of course there were sangha meetings that I also wanted to attend, and I wanted to eat as well. Eating is very important when you are expending so much energy. Also, I have to admit I wanted to have time to play tennis; it was something that I really enjoyed doing.

What can you accomplish in twenty minutes? Not much really unless you think about how over the course of a year that works out to more than 100 hours. I am sure that if you had 100 hours to spend on something you might be able to accomplish something very significatn. Yet how many of us waste our time thinking we don't have 100 hours when in fact we do. Over the years I was in the military alone I spent at least 400 hours reading and studying. Some nights I had more time, and some nights less but I actually kept a record and over the time I managed to be fairly consistent in my reading and study. This is a practice that has continued throughout my life.

The same can be said of our daily practice. One day a week I am in the detox unit of the hospital where I do most of my work. I spend an hour there teaching meditation to people of all ages who are cleaning their bodies out so they can hopefully go out and work on becoming clean and sober from addiction to drugs or alcohol. One of the reasons I do this is because scientists have studied the effects of meditation on the brain and on people with addictions. In one study they found that with a consistent meditation practice of 15-20 minutes a day for six weeks a measurable change takes place in the physical structure of the casing of the frontal lobe; the place of good decision making.

Twenty minutes a day, consistently day in and day out devoted to one thing is a very powerful and important way to get things done in our lives that we may not otherwise be able to accomplish. Are there things in your life you could apply the 20 minutes a day program to? Imagine developing a consistent daily practice of the Lotus Sutra every day for 20 minutes for a year or two years. For some of us it may mean returning to the first days of our practice, for others it may mean beginning. In many ways regardless whether we are new to the practice or long time practitioners we all can benefit from returning to the beginning. Perhaps we have become tired out along our journey and not even aware of being so.

What are the things that you find most frequently interfere with your practice and consequently your growth in life? Have you ever looked to see if there was a trend you could identify? For some people it is their personal arrogance that gets in the way of improvement; they already know everything. For others it is fear of failure. For some it might be simply insecurity. If we look deeply and honestly, we each have something that frequently lies at the heart of our limitations for growth. It might not be easy and certainly might not be pleasant to examine and admit to our tendencies. Yet being able to identify them gives us the ability to fully address them.

In addition to becoming tired out and wishing to return, the travelers were still afraid. Their guide had successfully lead them through roughly 250 days of travel finding them food and water because we are told in the gatha section that there was no water or grass along the way. So provisions either needed to be carried or provided. Yet they had survived thanks in part I am guessing to the skill of the guide. Yet even still they wanted to return home.

It is interesting how people will frequently abandon the very things that are indeed working toward. People in recovery will stop doing the things that are strengthening their sobriety. People will stop exercising or eating properly even though they have made and continue to make significant improvements in their health. People will stop studying and so their minds become inactive. People will abandon their Buddhist practice even though it has proven to be of great benefit in their lives. What are the things you abandon even while you can admit they are beneficial?

I struggle the most with eating healthily. Because of my basic metabolism I have never had an issue with gaining weight. In fact my problem is somewhat the reverse and I am unable to gain weight when I would like to. Because of this I am lulled into a false sense of being able to eat anything I wish. Over the years this has taken a toll on me and now I struggle with maintaining good levels of cholesterol and blood sugar. Even though I know eating better helps I get lazy and fall back into old habits of eating poorly.

Our group of travelers wish to return home even though they have succeeded so far. They have doubts and eventually the doubts cloud their ability to make a sound rational judgment. Over the years I have witnessed many people who have abandoned their Buddhist practice, sometimes to return to it again after a number of years away. Sometimes people turn their backs completely and never return

Discouragement

"The leader, who knew many expedients, thought, 'What a pity! They wish to go back without getting great treasures.' "
(Lotus Sutra, Chapter VII, page 227)

"He thought:
'How pitiful they are!
Why do they wish to return
Without getting great treasures?'
Thinking of an expedient, he said to himself:
'I will use my supernatural powers."
(Lotus Sutra, Chapter VII, page 234)

How many times have you been in the role similar to that of the leader of our group of travelers? Have you ever tried helping someone achieve their goal or dream only to have them abandon the effort or turn away before reaching their goal? What were your feelings at that time?

It has happened to me that I have tried to help someone along their path, either Buddhist or general life, and they have turned away at some point and abandoned their journey. It is a difficult thing to experience both on a personal level and thinking of the other person.

I have mentored teenagers and they were doing so well until something happened in their lives such as drugs or some big emotional let down. A life that was going one direction suddenly begins going off in a completely different direction and not one that leads to a good outcome. It is sad to see and experience.

But I wonder how much of the disappointment is feelings of personal failure. I know in all honesty for me there is that part. I have felt that somehow I have failed, that I wasn't skillful enough and that if I had only had one more skill or had done one more thing it might have turned out differently. I wonder if you have felt a similar thing in your life?

It is times such as those I wish I could have been as skillful as this leader or as the Buddha. But even the Buddha could not change the direction of the life of his cousin, Devadatta, who tried to destroy the Buddhist Sangha as well as kill the Buddha. There are times when I do believe that we can only do so much and then it is up to the individual to find his or her own path.

How much control of your life are you willing to give up in order to meet the goals of someone else? For most people there is a limit to how much of their personal identity and decision making they will give up before they rebel. I know I myself have limits, how about you? And so when you try to force someone to be as you think they should be they may become resentful and end up being driven further away rather than drawn closer.

I think here is a key point as you develop your own practice. It has to be your practice at a fundamental level. You can't practice for someone else trying to meet their standard. However your practice progresses it has to be your own style. Yes, in Nichiren Buddhism we have a framework of reciting the sutra and chanting Odaimoku but we do those things not so that we can all be identical. Likewise someone else needs to develop in their own way and they need to be allowed to do so with respect.

Some of my fondest memories of people are those who have guided me and helped in spite of the mistakes I made. The fact that I was allowed to make a mistake, suffer the consequence, and not be abandoned or judged were great life experiences for me. If we go back to the idea of aboutness, these instances were ones where I was able to learn more about my personal aboutness because someone else was secure in their own aboutness. It is often a person's own insecurity that causes them to be unable to let someone live their own life.

Your practice of Buddhism is not so that you will live a life exactly like the Buddha's. Your practice is to enable you to live your life as the Buddha did so that whatever you natural tendencies and specialties are they are so imbued with the spirit of enlightenment that you become the Buddha of your place, time, job, house and so forth. Your practice is about figuring out how Buddhism can enrich and inform your every day actions regardless of what your job or hobby or education or income level is.

One day a while back I received a phone call from a number I didn't recognize and from a place where I knew I had no friends. The voice on the other end of the phone identified himself as one of the young men I had mentored. He proceeded to tell me about how much he appreciated my efforts and how he had turned his life around and was now doing quite well. We never really know sometimes the profound impact we can have on people simply by not giving up and also by not forcing them to become exactly as we 'think' they should be. Of course not all stories end happily ever after.

It is a challenge to know when something shifts from being about the needs of the other person to our own personal need, and this is an important point. In the end we cannot live the life of another person no matter how hard we may try or how strong our desire is.

We are told the guide of our travelers employed skillful means in order to encourage the group to continue. It doesn't say he cajoled them or that he forced them or that he used any of the more common methods we might easily resort to. This is the trait of a good leader. I don't know about you, but there is still much for me to learn when it comes to being able to effectively employ skillful means.

What are the things that encourage you the most when you become discouraged? What is your personal style for becoming encouraged? Not everyone is equally encouraged by the same things. Some people like a pep talk; others like to be shown exactly what to do. Still others like a more hands off, leave me alone, approach from those who wish to help. But when you are discouraged are you also thinking that you can indeed do it and you are the most capable person to accomplish your goal?

Thinking you are the most capable person to solve your own problem is not an easy thing to remember or even believe. I suppose there might be an argument made that it isn't always the case, but I do believe that most of the time we are more capable than we give ourselves credit for. If you think about the truth of cause and effect though, no one else other than yourself made all the causes, which have resulted in the effects you experience, and it will fundamentally be up to you to unwind all of those effects. Perhaps this is a scary thought for you.

An experiment was done once where everyone in a group of people wrote their most serious problem on a slip of paper. All of the problems were then collected and read out. After all the problems were read out then each person was able to select a problem they would be willing to work on. Interestingly enough everyone chose their own problem. Every person in this experiment found their own problem to be the easiest one to solve and the one they would rather have than all the others. This was not necessarily a true scientific, controlled, experiment, but it was interesting in the results that it yielded.

While there might be some who would truly rather have another person's problems, I suspect that for many, their own problems would be more acceptable if they fully understood the nature and extent of other people's problems.

This is not to say that you are alone though in solving your problems. The trick is to seek out the best kind of support. I have mixed feelings about AA groups. There are some that are less harmful than others. Yet when it comes to recovery from addictions it is one of the best, as well as easily accessible support systems available in our society. There are other support groups as well such as Smart Recovery that a friend of mine participates in which for him is better than AA, but they are not so widely known or available.

The point though is that going it alone is the least likely way to succeed, whether it is in recovery or in other areas of our lives. It is true that you must walk the path yourself but there is no rule that you need to do it alone.

In my work with people in recovery, the people I see who repeatedly return to the detox unit are the ones who think they can do it alone and refuse to take advantage of resources available to them. Or they are people who for a while worked in community with others through various programs but at some point abandoned the effort and then tried to do it outside of community

We have a great resource in our practice of the Lotus Sutra. It doesn't promise you a smooth and easy life, but it does promise you the ability to work through your life problems and change yourself from within. If you think back on your life how frequently have you taken full advantage of resources when they

41

were available? Is it easier for you to try to do it on your own, and how does that work for you.

My truth may not be your truth. I do know that for me my practice of the Lotus Sutra has been a life changing experience. It hasn't happened overnight, it wasn't easy, nor was it smooth. In the end though I am much happier than I ever thought possible, and have accomplished more than I could have imagined. I wish the same and more for you.

I hope that you will continue to practice the Lotus Sutra, and chant Namu Myoho Renge Kyo until the end of your life. When you become discouraged I hope that you can think about the travelers on their journey and the fact that the place of unlimited treasures is only reached by completing the journey

The Magic City

"Having thought this, he expediently made a city by magic at a distance of three hundred yojanas from the starting-point of this dangerous road. He said to them, 'Do not be afraid! Do not go back! You can stay in that great city, and do anything you like. If you enter that city, you will be peaceful. If you go on afterwards and reach the place of treasures, then you can go home." (Lotus Sutra, Chapter VII, page 227)

"He made a great city by magic,
And adorned it with houses.
The city was surrounded by gardens, forests,
And by ponds and pools for bathing.
Many-storied gates and tall buildings [in that city]
Were filled with men and women.

Having made all this by magic,
He consoled the people, saying:
"Do not be afraid! Enter that city!
And do anything you like!"
(Lotus Sutra, Chapter VII, page 235)

If there were a magic city for you to do anything you wanted in, what is it that you would do?

By the time our group of travelers reach the magic city they have traveled 300 days out of a 500-day trip. They are more than half way along their path. As I think about this I am reminded of a labyrinth. At the center of many labyrinths there is a point of rest, there is a middle place that one travels along a path to reach.

When I spent a week at Mepkin Abbey near Charleston, SC they had a huge labyrinth out in one of their fields. I don't know exactly how large it was but I know that according to the pedometer I was wearing it was over one mile long one way. I was walking it at the end of the fall season so I could only imagine what it would look like in the summer or spring.

The paths were separated from each other by plantings of many different kinds of wildflowers. The flowers had all turned brown and were dying back for the winter hibernation but it did leave me to wonder at the beauty of it during the peak blooming season.

When you finally did reach the center there were benches to sit upon and reflect or meditate. I should point out that the plantings were high enough that as you traveled the path you felt walled in and in the center there was a real sense of being alone, and in the middle of nowhere.

The center was a place of rest and quiet. Yet the center is not the real destination because there is the journey outward again. In many ways the Magic City is like the center of a labyrinth. It is a place to renew and refresh but there still remains the outward journey.

When I imagine a magic city these folks are able to spend time in my original thoughts were of a castle type structure and one that would accommodate a group of a couple hundred or so travelers. In fact until I began working through the parable in more depth I really didn't focus on the size of the group. When I did it always seemed a rather intimate group of a not too large a number. In the prose section the number is simply stated as "many people," a rather vague number open to personal imagination. In the gatha section however it is given as "tens of millions of people."

There is quite a lot of room for different images to occur depending upon which version of the story you focus on.

If the group of travelers is tens of millions it would mean something like the entire population of Los Angeles or New York or Tokyo or some of the other major cities in the world all got up together and decided to move. This would hardly be an intimate group now would it? Yet even within a large city there are certainly people who know each other and might conceivably stay together. Think about your own real life situation for a moment. If you had to evacuate with your entire city or town, how many of your real life neighbors would do you know and could count upon for help? Are your friends or people you know very well living close by or do they live scattered all over the city? Do you imagine you would be able to travel with your friends if there were a mass evacuation?

My point in asking this is frequently it is the case that we do not know our neighbors and would indeed be traveling alone among relative strangers because we could not reach our friends easily. For me it is easy to talk to strangers and so over the years I know virtually all of my neighbors. When I am out walking my dog it frequently takes me much longer to complete the walk than it normally would because I stop and chat with people or as they drive by they slow their cars down and we talk for a few minutes. My father would frequently say that you should always be nice to people because you never know when you might be running for sheriff or when you might be running from the sheriff. Perhaps it is not the best of reasons for knowing people, but certainly good general advice.

How alone are you in your life? As I ask you to think about it, do you find it uncomfortable to think about? Do you find that your defense mechanism kicks in with various excuses for the reality you have created?

The life you live is almost certainly justifiable in your own mind; that is the nature of our minds. We are infinitely clever at constructing a plausible explanation or excuse for the way things are. It is much more difficult to look deeply and admit that the discomfort you experience on various levels is in fact something you created and actually is not what you may truly wish for. It may also be very difficult for you to do what is necessary to change things in your life so you can experience the kind of life you deeply wish it to be. Justifications and excuses are often our Magic City.

It is easy to take refuge in justifications and excuses. These are easy destinations to reach. The more difficult destination is one that has peeled away the illusions of justification and excuses. Has this ever been your experience, as painful or uncomfortable to admit as it may be?

Magic Cities can be very useful or they can be harmful. Depending upon the magic city you create in your own life you may find refreshing or you may find actually becomes a trap from which you cannot easily escape. I have employed the image of a labyrinth several times as I have written this. But suppose you are actually walking a maze. Mazes are tricky because they present the person with a lot of false choices leading to dead ends.

Frequently in literature the maze has other obstacles built in. Recently I was reading a fantasy book and the maze would cause the person to eventually forget who they were and why they were in the maze. Eventually the person would even forget they wished to exit. Finally they would starve to death because they would not have any food and would forget they were even hungry. But the maze is a construction created by the person because it was actually quiet easy to exit, if they could only remember.

When you fail to look critically at your life, your goals, your actions it is easy to get lost in a maze of forgetfulness and of illusions. This is one of the pitfalls of living a life of justification and excuses. Also when you think that something outside of yourself will solve the problem or change things in a fundamental way you have created an illusion that keeps you trapped in a dependent situation; always waiting on someone or something else to do something for you.

Buddhism is about wiping away the fog and illusion of these kinds of magic cities that trap you and prevent you from reaching enlightenment. The magic city in our story you will see is not a trap but a truly useful and beneficial occurrence.

Decision

"Thereupon the worn-out people had great joy. They said, 'We have never had such joy as this before. Now we shall be able to get off this bad road and become peaceful.'" (Lotus Sutra, Chapter VII, page 227)

There is no comparable part in the gathas for the selection in the sutra.

Simply the parable tells us that a Magic City appears and automatically the people declare their intent to go there. But it doesn't always happen that way in real life, and certainly not in the movies. There is almost always a group of people who oppose the most obvious solution, even if there is no compelling reason for the objection. Perhaps it is human nature that there will always be some who will function as the nay-sayers. Though, not all the time are nay-sayers obstructionists, they may indeed be serving as the conscience of the group. And, it is sometimes the case that they are the wise ones even though they may be in the minority.

I personally am skeptical of promises of great reward or instant benefit. That is why, as I said early on, when I came to the Lotus Sutra I was less apprehensive because I wasn't made unrealistic promises. In later years though that seemed to be the main selling message given to new people, that they could have all of their prayers answered if they only chanted some magic phrase. While I do believe that chanting Odaimoku can make it possible for wonderful things to happen in your life I believe that is only possible because of the changes that occur within your life. Perhaps I am too much of a rationalist.

I frequently provide support for people in the hospital and do witness many unexplainable instances of recovery. Yet unexplainable is not the same as no explanation. Simply because we cannot discern the cause of something does not mean it has no cause. All the things we witness or experience in our lives have causes, there is no effect that simply happens independent of a preceding cause. The changes that occur in our lives from chanting Odaimoku are the result of making a cause to the Lotus Sutra and the deeper that cause penetrates our being the greater and more profound the effect in our lives.

We may indeed be creating causes that impact the forces of nature, but I do believe it is ludicrous to believe that we can chant to make those causes and then continue to act against those causes and expect to be continually rewarded with benefit. If that were possible then addicts would potentially be the most happy people in the world, and yet in my work with people who have addictions to drugs and alcohol they are almost universally the least happy as they watch their magic city crumble around them.

As I read this section I can't help but wonder if the decision to go to the Magic City was unanimous and automatic. I wonder what the conversation within the group was like. What isn't told to us in this part of the Sutra? I would imagine that if it was something that suddenly appeared there would be a group of dissenters who would claim that this sudden appearance out of nothing could not be trusted. It reminds me of the caution authorities often dispense that if it is too good to be true it probably isn't.

Another possible argument would be that even by going to the magic city the rest of the journey still needs to be completed and no one knows what yet remains on that path. It might still be better to turn around and go back home.

Old ways are difficult to give up. Have you ever been faced with a situation and simply resigned yourself to continue as before because doing it the same way is easier? In a way this might be similar to the catch phrase that says the devil you know versus the devil you don't know.

Of course this ignores remembering the motivation for changing in the fist place. In our own lives we began practicing Buddhism for a particular reason, maybe it was to escape some unpleasant situation, or perhaps it was because of sadness or grief, there was some reason to begin this very strange religion. Well perhaps it isn't so strange now-a-days but way back in the 1960's it certainly was strange and part of the 'counter-culture.' So what was it that prompted you to begin practicing and studying the Lotus Sutra? Even if it was simply curiosity, that original curiosity has probably been satisfied, and yet you continue. So what is it that keeps you coming back?

For me the answer is because of the great joy I experience in my life through my practice. My practice has helped me to create the causes in my life that allow me to be peaceful and calm. I think about the passage from the Lotus Sutra that says those who practice will have lives which are peaceful and at ease. But it wasn't without making changes in my life, it didn't happen overnight, it wasn't easy, and frequently I made false turns.

Identifying the motivation for your practice can help you decided if indeed you have reached your destination? If you have not reached your destination then I wonder at the wisdom of abandoning the effort you have made to this day.

What are the arguments that spin around in your head when you are faced with doubts and discouragement? I am guessing that if you are anything like me there are parts of you that sometimes battle with each other about whether or not to continue or if this practice even works. I find it helpful to know what those inner parts sound like, what kinds of words they use, what strategy they employ. When I am intimate with those parts that try to discourage me and know the voices when they do pop up I know what they are and am better able to put those parts in their place.

Before you think I am crazy listening to voices in my head I will say that in Internal Family Systems (IFS) theory of therapy and psychological understanding the language is about parts. In this system it is said that we all have various parts which manifest in various ways. Now mind you, I am giving the very abbreviated version. But it is believed in this theory that while we each have many different parts to our selves at each of us lies a core self that tends toward compassion, connection, creativity, calmness, clarity and curiosity. If we think about the Ten Worlds then in a way we are not too far off from IFS. It is also interesting that many people frequently will say that a part of them feels some way, or a part of them thinks something, or even a part of them wants to do something but another part does not.

So as we travel our road to our destination of enlightenment we may frequently need a magic city to encourage us and to help us continue. We may experience various parts of ourselves that will doubt or become discouraged even as other parts still wish to continue. Again, knowing which parts are active and which parts are speaking can help us decide which to listen to. Is it the life condition of hell that draws you away, does your suffering part require you to continue suffering so it feels alive? Is it greed that keeps you from experiencing higher conditions of life, is there an itch in your life that continually need scratching and keeps you from being liberated?

These are all questions that will have different answers for each of us even though the questions may sound similar.

Resting

"Then they made their way forward and entered the magic city. They felt peaceful, thinking that they had already passed [through the bad road]." (Lotus Sutra, Chapter VII, page 227)

"They entered that city,
And had great joy.
They felt peaceful,
And thought that they had already passed [through the road]." (Lotus Sutra, Chapter VII, page 235)

The decision has been made and it appears from the sutra that they all went to the Magic City. But it seems that the folks have a false sense of what it is they have done. There is the feeling among the people that their journey may be finished even though we as the reader know otherwise.

As I read this my present journey to become a Board Certified Chaplain comes to mind. This has been a four year long effort on my part that has included many hours of education and a great many hours of clinical work. The most frustrating thing for me about the process has been the fact that on several occasions when I thought I had completed some requirement I later would find that yes I had done it but there was some other requirement that needed fulfilling. This would mean yet another set-back in the process and another task that would need to be accomplished even though no one said it needed to be done previously. It has at times been very discouraging. Even now as

I think I am finally at the last hurdle and ready to do the last part of the process I have strong doubts. So many things have popped up at the last minute that I fully expect something to rear its head and surprise me.

Life can be like that, in fact I suspect that for many people that is how their entire life seems. Thinking again about the image of the labyrinth you may notice that there are many times as you walk the labyrinth where you come very close to the center and then suddenly find yourself way far away on the outside.

There is another part of the labyrinth that I equate with the Magic City and that is the center. It is the center that represents in a way the completion of the journey and yet it isn't the end of the path because we need to exit the labyrinth. The center of the labyrinth is the point from which we reenter the world and take with us that which we have gained from our efforts. In this regard the Magic City and enlightenment have much in common.

We traditionally interpret the Magic City as the expedient rewards or benefits we experience along our path to enlightenment. Yet from the perspective that life continues beyond both the Magic City and enlightenment they both are similar because regardless whether it is the Magic City or enlightenment we must continue on with our lives. If we view enlightenment as some terminus point where our growth and development stops then we have a mistaken view of what enlightenment really is.

Enlightenment is not the end of life, nor it is a destination to reach where no further development is possible or desired. I believe that enlightenment is an ever moving ever deepening experience. If we think about the Buddha attaining enlightenment under the Bodhi tree we may feel that our own experience will be the same, that someday we will have a grand awakening and from that point forward all will be bliss. Yet I believe this ignores the development of the Buddha over the course of his enlightened life.

I believe that the Buddha's very own enlightenment continued to grow and develop over the course of many years, of all of his years until it finally reaches the point at which he could himself teach the Lotus Sutra. We frequently say that the Buddha withheld teaching the Lotus Sutra because the audience was not capable of understanding such a profound teaching. Yet there is a suspicion in my mind that it was also the case the Buddha himself was not capable of teaching it sooner. Of course I could be wrong but there really isn't any logical reason to suspect that enlightenment is some terminus point after which there is no more understanding possible.

To think that there is an ending destination actually deprives us of the possibility of infinity. Without infinity there would be no Eternal Buddha. Perhaps this is a stretch but no where else in human thinking or ability has there been an example of someone reaching the end of all understanding. I think it would be sad if that were the case because it would deprive each of us of uncovering a unique enlightenment in our own lives. There are infinite potentials for enlightenment and they all reside with the infinite number of ways life can manifest itself, of which humans only account for a relatively small amount.

How many times in your life have you reached a long sought after goal, sat back and sighed with relief, felt contented and thought all is right with the world? Maybe you have and maybe you were tempted to do those things but not too far off on the horizon you could clearly see that tomorrow would come and you would need to do something?

When I finally got discharged from the Marine Corps I was so relieved and happy. That feeling lasted quite a long time actually. Soon though, the awareness of the need to find some job occured. Even now as I have completed all the necessary educational training to be a chaplain I am very much relieved, in fact down right happy that the education part is all finished, yet I am aware that I still need to complete an additional 2000 hours of clinical work before my goal is reached.

Heck when I graduated from high school I felt so excited at being finished with school. Yet there was college after that, and at various points in my life other educational obligations and requirements popped up. So high school graduation was only one milestone but not the end of the process of learning.

Getting a nice job has frequently been celebrated only to realize that many new things had to be learned and many responsibilities fulfilled. The birth of a child is quite an exciting occasion, but the excitement is only the beginning of the real responsibility of providing for and raising the new born. The satisfaction of a day of good hard productive work soon melts away with the dawning of the next sunrise and the reality that life goes ever onward.

I've already talked about magic cities we may construct that are harmful to us yet in a way any magic city is harmful if we consider it as the final resting place from all of our efforts. Also if we consider enlightenment as a place of final rest then it too becomes merely a magic city, a trap in fact.

In some literature there are accounts of islands or places where people are led to where time stops and the person becomes trapped and years go by before the eventually return to the world they left behind. To the individual it may seem like only a few hours or a few days when in fact it might have been hundreds of years. Our own individually constructed magic cities can also trap us in both good and harmful ways. Part of our process of becoming enlightened is to be able to discern reality from fiction.

The teachings in the Lotus Sutra can guide us because they really do speak to the reality of our lives. We study the Lotus Sutra not just to discover what it can be like but to also discern what we are like in this moment and what needs to be done to change. I have said before the first step in changing our lives is to understand what needs to be changed. If you are more than comfortable in hell then it is most unlikely you will seek to discover other options. Being aware of suffering and being aware of other possibilities awakens within us the idea that other ways of living and experiencing life are possible.

The Lotus Sutra provides us with a window to see other possibilities for our lives and it also provides us with a map that we can use to get to those other ways of being. This is one reason I choose the Parable of the Magic City to write at length about.

Pulling Back the Curtain

"Seeing that they had already had a rest and relieved their fatigue, the leader caused the city to disappear, and said to them, 'Now the place of treasures is near. I made this city by magic in order to give you a rest." (Lotus Sutra, Chapter VII, page 227)

"Seeing that they had already had a rest,
The leader collected them, and said:
'Go on ahead now!
This is a magic city.
You were tired out halfway.
You wished to go back.
Therefore, I made this city by magic
As an expedient.
Make efforts!
Let us go to the place of treasures!'"
(Lotus Sutra, Chapter VII, page 235-236)

I'm not sure how you would feel if all the sudden this restful and peaceful place you had stayed in disappeared from you. I suppose though that in one way or another we all have experienced something similar in our lives. I am guessing that there have been times when you thought something was secure, or that it was permanent only to have it change and vanish. Hopefully it wasn't harmful to you.

Generally when I teach this section of the parable I compare the Magic City to the many benefits we experience along our journey towards an enlightened life. But in this writing as I examine it more deeply it does seem that the city disappearing is rather harsh, perhaps it would be better if it gradually faded away. No, I guess that wouldn't be good either.

Perhaps my reluctance to the city vanishing is an indication of the power and lure of the Magic City. Wouldn't it be nice if all of our Magic Cities were permanent? Are you finding at this point any resistance to the notion of the disappearance of the Magic City? Maybe you are not and maybe it is just me because I have been thinking of this so much. Oh well, it really is time to let it go.

Now we all know the Magic City is only a temporary condition, as is actually all of our life experiences. In many ways our lives are a series of Magic Cities connected by roads to travel to those Magic Cities. Whether what we experience is a joyful occurrence or a troublesome occurrence, because of the impermanence of all things they will not last forever.

Of course depending upon our lives we can create conditions for the continual occurrence of similar experiences. If we are suffering and we fail to properly understand the true nature of our suffering or the causes we are making then we may indeed be creating the kind of life dominated by suffering.

It is the message of the Lotus Sutra and Buddhism that we do not need to be a victim of suffering, that indeed there is a way to extricate ourselves from lives that wander from one suffering to another. With the Lotus Sutra as our guide we can leave the places of trouble in our lives and gradually change our lives to become ones in which joy and happiness are the predominant experiences. Notice I said predominant, because every life will experience trials and tribulations. But with lives firmly rooted in the Lotus Sutra we can safely navigate those upsetting phenomena just as our band of merry travelers were eventually able to reach their destination.

Notice that in the Lotus Sutra even after the Magic City has been removed the group of people still needed to continue on their journey. It is the same in our lives, it is the same with enlightenment, just as it is with the labyrinth. We reach the center, but we need to leave. We need to re-enter the world and the challenge is what will we take with us.

In this parable we are not told anything at all about the final destination other than it is a place of unlimited treasure. I began this writing by exploring what is not written. Here what we are not told is what life was like for this group of travelers once they reached their destination.

It is my experience as well as what I have witnessed working with people, that frequently little thought is given to what comes after a goal is reached. Sometimes we may indeed think beyond the goal, but most of the time the focus is on the goal and then what follows is left to unfold as it may.

As I prepare for and enter a life in retirement I have been very much consumed with thinking about what that will be like. Since the demarcation for my retirement will occur no matter what, I cannot stop the aging process and I had determined that by a certain age I would enter retirement. Now what I have been preparing for is what retirement would mean to me, what I would do, how I would live, how I would support myself, and how I would prepare to die.

As my life journey nears its ending it seems most appropriate to think about how I want that to happen, or at least what I wish it to be like since none of us can be absolutely certain or control our death. As I engage in this process I can honestly say that at no other time in my life do I recall giving as much thought to the future beyond the destination.

I wonder how is it for you? Do you tend to focus on the goal so much that what comes after the attainment of the goal slips from your thought process?

I wonder what life was like for this group of travelers when they got to their destination. If they are like immigrants throughout history they will need to find places to live, perhaps occupations to support themselves, even schools for the children, and places to shop and worship. It is pretty neat as I think about it how ordinary the extraordinary can be at times. Do you ever experience that?

Conclusion

"Now the place of treasures is near. I made this city by magic in order to give you a rest." (Lotus Sutra, Chapter VII, page 227)

I hope that this little book has provided you with several things. One, I hope it has perhaps shown you a different way of approaching and understanding the Lotus Sutra. Two, perhaps it has revealed to you a mirror of your own life as found in the Lotus Sutra. Finally, I hope it has given you some hope and courage through the model of our travelers for your own spiritual journey.

I began this book talking about the tradition among Jewish scholars of midrash, the exploration of what is not written in the Torah. When I began I wasn't sure how well the example of midrash would fit with the study of the Lotus Sutra. In many ways the exploration of the parable of the Magic City was a journey into a journey. As I said in my final section I was amazed at how reluctant I was to leave the Magic City when it came time to wrap up my writing. I had grown quite attached to the journey getting there and finally reaching it I was let down when I had to leave and move on.

Even knowing that moving on meant the attainment of my goal did not help with my grief at the journey ending. By remaining in the Magic City it meant that I would not have to conclude this writing. So the Magic City became a safe place from which to avoid further activity. I share this observation with you the reader to show how it is possible for us to find Magic Cities in many places, even unexpected places, in our lives.

There is another meditative or spiritual practice I would like to introduce to you from a different religious tradition and that is lectio divina. There are many ways to practice lectio divina however the one I would like to tell you about is a slight variation to what was traditionally practiced in Christian monasteries.

One way of studying the sutra in general and this parable in specific is to begin your meditation perhaps by chanting the Odaimoku for a short period of time. At the conclusion of your chanting continue sitting and slowly read through the parable. After you have read through the parable then pick any character within that story and imagine yourself as that character or person. Now go back over the selection and think about how your character would respond or what they would be doing or saying. Look around you in your mind and see the other characters from your character's point of view and imagine interacting with them as your identified character. See if you are relating to the selection in a new and different way now that you are examining it from a different perspective.

Perhaps you might also incorporate the idea of filling in what isn't in the story but you find missing and wish to explore. The possibilities are endless and each exploration into the selection can teach you something new. Perhaps over the period of several days look at the same selection from different perspectives. As part of your meditation practice become curious about yourself and ask why you chose that character today, is there some lesson you needed to learn from that character? Perhaps even there is some aversion to a different character and so you chose not to become them; be curious.

As I mentioned early on the Lotus Sutra is not a story about anyone so much as it is the actual story of your life. The more we can merge our lives and the truth in the Lotus Sutra the more aboutness we will have and the truths will no longer be separated.

At the end of this book I have provided some suggestions on how to study the Lotus Sutra, you may find helpful. Feel free to customize it to your own liking, it is merely a template, it isn't the rule. Also, for those who may be interested in a structured outline I have given a series of exercises to be carried out over a period of time. Different people like different things so if you don't find this helpful then please ignore it. Some people like things more directed and so perhaps they will find these tools helpful. Again, take what you need and what you find useful and leave the rest.

"Make efforts!
Let us go to the place of treasures!"
(Lotus Sutra, Chapter VII, page 236)

Thank you for reading my book. Let us together make great efforts to attain enlightenment and share our joy with others.

With Gassho,
Ryusho

Study Guide

I would like to offer you a strategic way you might want to use when you are studying the Lotus Sutra. You may or may not find it a useful tool, that is alright. Perhaps it will help you develop a tool for yourself. However it may be nice place to begin.

First of course is to select the passage you wish to study. You may do this by going systematically from the beginning of the sutra to the end working your way through a select number of pages each day or week. You might also just decide you want to focus on one parable at a time. However you choose to plan out your study, try to actually have a plan and stick with it. Remember a large accumulation of wisdom from the Sutra begins with a steady approach of small additions.

I. Read the selection.

First of course is to read the selection. Take your time reading. On this first read just enjoy the experience of reading the Buddha's words and letting them be absorbed by your life; just open up to feelings and not understandings. You may feel nothing but confusion, that is perfectly acceptable, as acceptable as being blown away by the awe and mystery of the sutra.

II. Observation - What does the selection say?

Now you are going to take a much closer look at the details. You might consider answering some of these questions.
a. Who are the people involved?
b. What happened?
c. What ideas are being expressed?
d. What resulted?
e. Who is the speaker?
f. What is the purpose?
g. What is the stated reason?

h. How are things accomplished? How well? How quickly? By what method?
i. Are there key words in the passage?
j. What images are in the passage?

III. Interpretation - **What does it mean?**

Write down questions about what you don't understand in the passage.
What do you think the passage meant to the original audience that received the teachings?
In light of its meaning to the original audience, what does it mean to you?
Are there words you need to look up and understand better?
Finally, what is a single primary meaning of this passage for you now (this may change over time).

IV. Illustration - **How can I pass this on?**

Draw a picture, or diagram, or write a word picture, or in some other way illustrate what you have discovered from this passage. You might even compose a poem or write something in your journal. Doing these types of things helps you make the story or teaching your own. The more you own it the easier it will be for you to live it and share it.

V. Application - **What do I need to do?**

The following questions may help you apply this passage to your life.

1. Is there something for me to avoid, i.e. doing, thinking
2. Is there a promise for me to claim?
3. Is there an example for me to follow? or not follow?
4. What knowledge have I gained? Is there other knowledge I should pursue?

Lectio Divina

Besides modeling this exploration of the Parable of the Magic City on the Jewish scholarly tradition of midrash I also employed a form of lectio divina from Christian traditions. I was first introduced to lectio divina while I was studying to become a chaplain. Every morning when I stayed at the Trappist monastery, Mepkin Abbey, near Charleston, SC lectio divina was a part of their early morning services.

The first morning service is Vigils at 3:20AM. Following Vigils was one half hour of meditation and then at 4:30AM was Lectio Divina for thirty minutes. The lectio divina as practiced by the monks was done in private so I am unsure as to how they engaged in the practice. I did learn from one of the novice monks that it was done individually and not as a group activity. I am unable to share with you the actual structure of their lectio divina practice.

If you are inclined to investigate lectio divina for yourself you will discover there are many formats for this practice and it can be done individually as well as in group. I will share with you a form of lectio divina that I used to a modified degree for this writing but one I frequently use on a more personal practice level.

Before you begin the process determine which selection of the Lotus Sutra, or even Nichiren's writing you will be focussing on. I would suggest that you make this a multi-day practice, perhaps even a week long for one single selection. You might begin on a Sunday and continue to work with the same passages until Saturday, for example.

Once you determine the selection you will be working with I recommend chanting Odaimoku for a while. Then after you conclude chanting, while still seated in front of the mandala or in your sacred space read through the selection you have chosen. Read it slowly and carefully, paying attention to all of the words, punctuation, every detail of the physical presentation of the selection.

After you have finished reading through your selection, and you might even consider reading it out loud. Actually hearing yourself read it can have a different impact on your life from reading it silently inside your head. After you have finished reading pick one character from the selection. It might be the person speaking whether it is the narrator or one of the subjects of the selection, possibly even an unknown recipient of the writing.

Now go deeply into that character asking yourself what they are seeing in this scene, what might they be experiencing. Go as deeply exploring as much detail as you possibly can. Using the eyes and ears of the character and not your own describe or contemplate what they see, what they hear, what they smell, what they might be thinking. Try to experience this from their perspective and not your own.

Perhaps it is a letter Nichiren wrote to one of his followers. Imagine receiving this letter. Remember it will be in the format of a scroll, more than likely if it is long. What would it be like unrolling a portion at a time to read this letter to yourself? Try to soak up as many details as possible. If you are reading the Lotus Sutra, you might look around you at the others in the congregation, is the Buddha speaking to you or is he speaking to your neighbor or someone way on the other side? What are your reactions to what the Buddha is saying.

Depending upon the character you choose you may be the main person or you might be a bystander. You might even be the Buddha speaking to someone in the assembly. You might even be some supernatural deity who is raining madarava flowers on the Buddha. This is why I recommend spending several days on one selection. Every day assume some new person in the story or spend several days as the same person, either way try to experience the selection from as many different perspectives as possible. It could possibly take you a month to work through one small portion of the Lotus Sutra or Nichiren writing.

Every time you engage in this practice be aware of what you are experiencing and feeling more than you are aware of meanings or interpretations of concepts. This is intended to be primarily an experiential activity and not an intellectual process. The intellectual understanding will follow in a much more personal way through this experiencing of the sutra or gosho.

Also as part of the practice be curious about why today you chose to be a particular character or subject. Let nothing you experience go unexamined, there are lessons and messages to be found in even the smallest detail. Be less concerned with reaching a conclusion and greatly open to being as curious as you possibly can.

After you spend your time exploring as above then spend some time chanting Odaimoku letting your experience seep deeply into your body. You may feel a need to process what you experienced and that is alright but it isn't necessary. I would recommend though avoiding rushing the conclusion as it can have a dampening affect on the process of deep assimilation of the experience. That is why allowing yourself some time to chant Odaimoku is important. This should begin and end with chanting to your hearts content. As I frequently say don't chant until a certain time has elapsed but chant until your life is full.

I hope you try engaging in the type of lectio divina practice. As you do it more you may wish to modify it to your own personality. It is perfectly acceptable to change things to enable you to gain the most benefit. Being childlike with great curiosity is an excellent way to approach the Dharma.

Labyrinths

In my work as a hospital chaplain I have had many opportunities to use labyrinths in the work of providing spiritual care to patients. There seems to be something about working a labyrinth that is calming and soothing. Perhaps because it is an easily grasped metaphor for our experiences in life. The history of labyrinths goes back to prehistory times and they can be found in virtually all cultures in one form or another. In a way circumambulations are a form of labyrinth.

When we circumambulate the Buddha we have an entry point, the point at which we approach the statue in the center.

First we bow to the Buddha by placing our forehead on the ground at his feet. We place our hands on the floor beside our head with the palms facing upward. We then raise our hands beside our ears as if we were picking the Buddha up by his feet and elevating him above ourselves. We do this supplication not as beggars entreating some deity to bestow gifts or rewards. Instead we do this to show our great appreciation to the teacher who leads us to enlightenment. We are humble and appreciative in front of our great teacher.

Then we begin walking around the Buddha in a clockwise direction always keeping our right shoulder towards the Buddha. We walk completely around the Buddha, even behind the statue. We can see all aspects of the Buddha from every angle. We are so very close to the Buddha, but we are not quite there yet. Our aspiration to attain enlightenment just as the Buddha is strengthened by our close proximity to the Buddha. There is nothing that is not revealed to us as we continue our walk.

We always keep our right shoulder facing the Buddha because that is the shoulder we uncover, it is the traditional weapon shoulder. We come to the Buddha bear, and vulnerable. But we are safe in the presence of the Buddha because the Buddha only wishes us to be like himself.

Our walking around the Buddha benefits us greatly as we empty our mind and leave behind all of the cares and concerns of the mundane world. We are in a sacred space it is just us and the Buddha. It is up to us to continue our mindful walk in the presence of this great example of how to live.

If we think of the great Bodhisattvas that rose up from the ground who approached the Buddha and rather than asking for reward or benefit they asked if the Buddha was in good health. Our benefits come to us in the same manner. They come not because we ask for them or because we have done anything special. They come because we think of nothing else except how we can enable others to attain what the Buddha has taught us. The great Bodhisattvas from underground asked first of the Buddha and then they began to circumambulate.

Our actions of circumambulation come directly out of the Lotus Sutra. We continue to practice as Bodhisattvas from beneath the ground. The work of the labyrinth is in many ways similar to this very ancient practice in the Lotus Sutra. Even as we perform the circumambulations around the Buddha at some point we need to carry out our vow to the Buddha to go into the Saha world and teach others of the great joy of practicing the Lotus Sutra. Just as in the labyrinth there is the going in and then coming out.

The objective in labyrinth work is not the getting to the center but the taking out of the center what we learned and experienced and bringing it with us as we exit and return to the mundane world.

I am including images of a few labyrinths which you may find helpful. There are countless versions of labyrinths from very simple to extremely complex. In all cases the principle and symbolism is the same. You may even decide to go on the web and print out some copies for you to keep handy. Or you might, as I have done, get a finger labyrinth to carry with you so you can always do labyrinth work wherever you are. I have several styles and sizes. I find them very contemplative.

In this section of the study guide I have compiled all of the various questions I have posed throughout this book. Here you c an find them all in one hand location. Perhaps you may find them useful as you construct your own interpretation of the Parable of the Magic City.

Questions

In this section of the study guide I have compiled all of the various questions I have posed throughout this book. Here you can find them all in one hand location. Perhaps you may find them useful as you construct your own interpretation of the Parable of the Magic City.

Before the Journey

Do you consider how you begin something? - Setting one's intention either as we start an activity or as we engage in the activity can help remind us what it is we really hope to accomplish.

How do we know about the place of unlimited treasure? - Perhaps ask yourself how did you hear about Nichiren Shu?

How did the travelers meed up with each other? - How do you find the people you need in your life?

What motivated the travelers? - What motivates you?

We can of course say that they represent the Bhiksus and their quest for enlightenment, but how can we read this in our own lives?

How is it that you developed a seeking or questing to learn and practice Buddhism? - For now spend some time in introspection on the reasons you began the search for and the practice of Buddhism.

What was or is going on in your life that draws you to your practice and motivates you to continue day after day?

Over time those treasures we seek change and mutate, some may even disappear because we are no longer interested in such things. How have things changed for you over the course of your practice?

When you finally decided to explore or even practice Buddhism can you recall what it was that really convinced you to take up the faith in earnest?

One thing we are not told is how these people came together. How was it they found each other, or decided collectively to undertake this journey? Can you imagine?

Considering this for a moment you might ask yourself the age old question of whether you are a spiritual being living an ordinary life or an ordinary person living a spiritual life?

Spend some time in introspection on the reasons you began the search for and the practice of Buddhism.

The Guide

So you make your decision using your set of criteria for your own individual reasons but how do you decide upon who will guide you?

How did you decide that practicing the Lotus Sutra was or is the correct path for you to follow?

If you were merely seeking out Buddhism in general, there are countless ways in which to engage in Buddhist practice and develop your Buddhist aboutness. What was it about the Lotus Sutra that caught your attention?

How do people make such life and death decisions?

Thinking about your own life, have there been times when you have had to make a very important decision?

What criteria did you use to base your decision?

How do you decide among frequently many options which course of action to take? Do you have any basic criteria, or do you just wing it?

What is your method of problem solving, have you even ever considered it?

Are there places in your life where you experience a discord between what you know you should do, or you want to do and what you actually end up doing?

If you are like most people, there are probably areas where you don't live up to your greatest expectations. What do we do in situations like this?

Who are some of the wise people you have had in your life?

I know why I continue to follow the teachings of the Buddha but I wonder what motivates you to keep going?

What has gotten you through the tough times in the past?

There are lessons we can learn from the heroic journeys of myth and legend, and this parable is one example. - What lessons can you learn from this or other heroic journeys?

I encourage each of you to re-examine your lives and your thinking. Ask yourself if you are valuing your life from the perspective of victory or winning. Do you truly value all of your experiences and efforts from the perspective that no effort in Buddhism is wasted?

Does the hero find the guide or the guide find the hero?

Which is really the hero, the guide or the one making the journey?

The Journey

Have you ever considered the role your obstacles play in your growth and movement to enlightenment?

We like things to be familiar, predictable, comfortable, which of course means that we are more inclined to stagnate and also suffer. Not everyone is this way of course but generally this is true. Is this true for you? Honestly?

What are you clinging to that may be causing suffering?

I wonder if you remember what your goals for this year were on January first. Do you, as part of your life process, make personal goals, listing things you wish to achieve over periods of time?

I wonder what changes you could accomplish in your life if you made a commitment from today for 500 days to practice on a regular consistent basis towards the achievement of some change in your life?

Would you be able to travel the entire 500 days without giving up or abandoning or forgetting your goal and effort?

What can you accomplish in twenty minutes?

Twenty minutes a day, consistently day in and day out devoted to one thing is a very powerful and important way to get things done in our lives that we may not otherwise be able to accomplish. Are there things in your life you could apply the 20 minutes a day program to?

What are the things that you find most frequently interfere with your practice and consequently your growth in life?

Have you ever looked to see if there was a trend you could identify?

What are the things you abandon even while you can admit they are beneficial?

Discouragement

How many times have you been in the role similar to that of the leader of our group of travelers?

Have you ever tried helping someone achieve their goal or dream only to have them abandon the effort or turn away before reaching their goal?

What were your feelings at that time?

How much control of your life are you willing to give up in order to meet the goals of someone else?

What are the things that encourage you the most when you become discouraged?

What is your personal style for becoming encouraged?

The Magic City

If there were a magic city for you to do anything you wanted in, what is it that you would do?

Think about your own real life situation for a moment. If you had to evacuate with your entire city or town, how many of your real life neighbors would do you know and could count upon for help?

Are your friends or people you know very well living close by or do they live scattered all over the city?

Do you imagine you would be able to travel with your friends if there were a mass evacuation?

How alone are you in your life?

As I ask you to think about it, do you find it uncomfortable to think about? Do you find that your defense mechanism kicks in with various excuses for the reality you have created?

Magic Cities can be very useful or they can be harmful. Depending upon the magic city you create in your own life you may find refreshing or you may find actually becomes a trap from which you can not easily escape. Think about your Magic City.

Decision

As I read this section I can't help but wonder if the decision to go to the Magic City was unanimous and automatic. I wonder what the conversation within the group was like. What isn't told to us in this part of the Sutra?

Have you ever been faced with a situation and simply resigned yourself to continue as before simply because doing it the same way is easier?

So what was it the prompted you to begin practicing and studying the Lotus Sutra?

Even if it was simply curiosity, I wonder if you have completely satisfied that curiosity, and yet you continue. So what is it that keeps you coming back?

Identifying the motivation for your practice can help you decided if indeed you have reached your destination?

If you have not reached your destination then I wonder at the wisdom of abandoning the effort you have made to this day.

What are the arguments that spin around in your head when you are faced with doubts and discouragement?

Is it the life condition of hell that draws you away, does your suffering part require you to continue suffering so it feels alive?

Is there an itch in your life that continually need scratching and keeps you from being liberated?

Resting

How many times in your life have you reached a long

sought after goal, sat back and sighed with relief, felt contented and thought all is right with the world?

Maybe you have and maybe you were tempted to do those things but not too far off on the horizon you could clearly see that tomorrow would come and you would need to do something?

Pulling Back the Curtain

Wouldn't it be nice if all of our Magic Cities were permanent. Are you finding at this point any resistance to the notion of the disappearance of the Magic City?

Do you tend to focus on the goal so much that what comes after the attainment of the goal slips from your thought process?

I wonder what life was like for this group of travelers when they got to their destination. If they are like immigrants throughout history they will need to find places to live, perhaps occupations to support themselves, even schools for the children, and places to shop and worship. It is pretty neat as I think about it how ordinary the extraordinary can be at times. Do you ever experience that?

Text of the Parable of the Magic from the Lotus Sutra

"I will tell you a parable. Once upon a time there was a dangerous, bad road five hundred yojanas long. It was so fearful that no men lived in the neighborhood. Now many people wished to pass through this road in order to reach a place of treasures. They were led by a man, clever, wise, and well informed of the conditions of the dangerous road. He took them along this dangerous road, but halfway the people got tired of walking. They said to him, 'We are tired out. We are also afraid of the danger of this road. We cannot go a step farther. Our destination is still far off. We wish to go back.'

"The leader, who knew many expedients, thought, 'What a pity! They wish to go back without getting great treasures.' Having thought this, he expediently made a city by magic at a distance of three hundred yojanas from the starting-point of this dangerous road. He said to them, 'Do not be afraid! Do not go back! You can stay in that great city, and do anything you like. If you enter that city, you will be peaceful. If you go on afterwards and "reach the place of treasures, then you can go home.'

"Thereupon the worn-out people had great joy. They said, 'We have never had such joy as this before. Now we shall be able to get off this bad road and become peaceful.'

"Then they made their way forward and entered the magic city. They felt peaceful, thinking that they had already passed [through the bad road]. Seeing that they had already had a rest and relieved their fatigue, the leader caused the city to disappear, and said to them, 'Now the place of treasures is near. I made this city by magic in order to give you a rest.'
(Lotus Sutra, Chapter VII, pages 226 & 227)

"Suppose there was a bad and dangerous road.
Many wild animals lived in the neighborhood.
No man was there; no water nor grass there.
The road was so fearful.

Many tens of millions of people
Wished to pass through this dangerous road.
The road was very long.
It was five hundred yojanas long.

The people had a leader.
He had a good memory.
He was wise and resolute in mind.
He could save people from dangers.

Getting tired,
The people said to him:
"We are tired.
We wish to go back."

He thought:
'How pitiful they are!
Why do they wish to return
Without getting great treasures?'
Thinking of an expedient, he said to himself:
'I will use my supernatural powers.'

He made a great city by magic,
And adorned it with houses.
The city was surrounded by gardens, forests,
And by ponds and pools for bathing.
Many-storied gates and tall buildings [in that city]
Were filled with men and women.

Having made all this by magic,

He consoled the people, saying:
"Do not be afraid! Enter that city!
And do anything you like!"

"They entered that city,
And had great joy.
They felt peaceful,
And thought that they had already passed [through the road].

Seeing that they had already had a rest,
The leader collected them, and said:
"Go on ahead now!
This is a magic city.
You were tired out halfway.
You wished to go back.
Therefore, I made this city by magic
As an expedient.

"Make efforts!
Let us go to the place of treasures!"
(Lotus Sutra, Chapter VII, pages 234-236)

How to Draw Your Own Labyrinth

The 7-circuit labyrinth is drawn as shown. To draw an 11-circuit labyrinth, add an "L" in each corner and follow the same plan as for 7:

How to begin an 11-circuit labyrinth

Connect with Ryusho Jeffus online:

Twitter: @ryusho @myoshoji

Facebook:
https://www.facebook.com/Ryusho

Blog: www.myoshoji.org/blog

Made in the USA
Columbia, SC
27 January 2025